Contents

Beaded Hat and Scarf

■■□□

Measurements

Hat
- **Head circumference** 19"/48cm
- **Length** 9"/23cm

Scarf
- Approximately 5½ x 65"/14 x 165cm

Gauge

15 sts and 25 rows to 4"/10cm over St st using size 10 (6mm) needles and one strand each of A and B held together.
Take time to check your gauge.

Stitch Glossary

PB (place bead) Push pre-strung bead up to front of work snug against last st worked and knit or purl, drawing bead through st being worked.

pfb Purl into front and back of st for an inc 1.

Notes

1 Hat and scarf are worked with one strand each of A and B held tog throughout.
2 Beads are pre-strung on A and placed when instructed.
3 Hat is worked from side to side with short row shaping. Crown is picked up and knit along short row edge. Ribbing is picked up along unshaped edge. Purl side of hat is RS.

Hat

With sewing needle, thread 60 beads on A. With one strand each of A and B held tog, cast on 29 sts.
Row 1 (WS) Knit. **Row 2** P9, PB, p9, PB, p9.
Row 3 Knit. **Row 4 short row** P17, turn. **Row 5 short row** Knit to end of row—mark this edge.
Row 6 P4, PB, [p9, PB] twice, p4. **Row 7** Knit.
Row 8 Purl.
Rep rows 1–8 until piece measures 19"/48cm from beg along marked edge, end with a row 7.

What you'll need:

YARN (1) (3)
1¾oz/50g, 450yd/415m of any lace weight mohair blend in teal (A)
5¼oz/150g, 415yd/375m of any DK weight wool blend in dark teal (B)

KNITTING NEEDLES
One pair size 10 (6mm) needles *or size to obtain gauge*

ADDITIONAL MATERIALS
300 size 3mm-4mm glass E beads in brass—60 for hat, 240 for scarf
Sewing needle to fit through bead opening
Stitch markers

Bind off 28 sts. Do not fasten off—1 st rem on needle.

Crown

With RS facing and last st on needle, pick up and k 39 sts evenly along unmarked edge of hat—40 sts.
Next row (WS) Knit. **Next (dec) row** *P2 tog; rep from * to end—20 sts rem.
Rep dec row once more—10 sts rem.
Cut yarn leaving long tail. Thread yarn through rem sts and draw tight.

Ribbing

With RS facing, pick up and k 58 sts evenly along marked edge of hat.
Row 1 (WS) P2, * k2, p2; rep from * across.
Row 2 K2, *p2, k2; rep from * across.
Rep rows 1 and 2 once more and row 1 once.
Bind off loosely in pat. Cut yarn leaving a long tail for sewing. Sew seam.

Scarf

With sewing needle, thread 50 beads on A. With one strand each of A and B held tog, cast on 304 sts.

Ribbed Edge

Rows 1-6 *K2, p2; rep from * across.
Next (dec) row (RS) K1, k2 tog, [k3, k2 tog] 60 times, k1—243 sts rem.
Knit 1 row.

Beaded Section

Note When 50 beads have been placed, break A, thread 50 beads more and rejoin A.
Row 1 (RS) P5, pm, k to last 5 sts, pm, p5.
Row 2 K5, sl marker (sm), p to 2nd marker, sm, k5. Cont to slip markers every row. **Row 3** K6, [PB, k9] 23 times, PB, k6. **Row 4** P6, [PB, p9] 23 times, PB, p6. **Row 5** Knit. **Row 6** Rep Row 2.
Row 7 P5, k6, [PB, k9] 22 times, PB, k6, p5.
Row 8 K5, p6, [PB, p9] 22 times, PB, p6, k5.
Row 9 Knit. **Row 10** Purl.
Row 11 Rep Row 3. **Row 12** K5, p1, [PB, p9] 23 times, PB, p1, k5.
Row 13 Rep row 1, slipping markers.
Row 14 Rep row 2. **Row 15** K11, [PB, k9] 22 times, PB, k11. **Row 16** P11, [PB, p9] 22 times, PB, p11. **Row 17** Knit.
Row 18 Rep Row 2. **Row 19** P5, k1, [PB, k9] 23 times, PB, k1, p5. **Row 20** Rep Row 12. **Row 21** Knit. **Row 22** Purl.

Ribbed Edge

Next row (RS) Purl 1 row.
Next (inc) row (WS) P1, pfb, [k3, pfb] 60 times, p1—304 sts.
Next 6 rows *K2, p2; rep from * across.
Bind off in pat.

Leaf Hat and Mittens

■◻◻

Sizes

Hat and mittens sized for Adult Woman.

Measurements

Hat
- Circumference stretched 20"/51cm
- Length 9"/23cm

Mittens
- Hand circumference 7"/18cm
- Length 11½"/29cm

Gauge

14 sts and 20 rnds to 4"/10cm over St st using larger needles.
Take time to check your gauge.

Hat

With smaller circular needle, cast on 76 sts. Join, taking care not to twist sts. Place marker (pm) for beg of rnd and slip marker every rnd.

Next (rib) rnd *[K1, p2] 6 times, k1; rep from * three times more.

Rep rib rnd until piece measures 2"/5cm from beg.

Change to larger circular needle.

Next (set-up) rnd [K7, pm, p2, k1, p2, pm, k7] 4 times.

Beg Chart (see page 32)

Note Stitch count changes in chart rnds.

Next rnd [K to marker, sl marker, work chart rnd 1, sl marker] 4 times, work to end of rnd. Cont to work chart in this manner through rnd 8. Rep rnds 1–8 once more, then rnds 1–5 once—84 sts in rnd.

Shape Crown

Note Change to dpn when sts no longer fit on

What you'll need:

Hat
YARN (4)
3½oz/100g, 110yd/101m of any bulky weight variegated wool

KNITTING NEEDLES
One each sizes 9 and 10½ (5.5 and 6.5mm) circular needles, 24"/60cm long *or size to obtain gauge*
One set (5) size 10½ (6.5) double-pointed needles (dpns)

Mittens
YARN (5)
3½oz/100g, 110yd/101m of any bulky weight variegated wool

KNITTING NEEDLES
One set (5) each size 9 and 10½ (5.5 and 6.5) double-pointed needles (dpns) *or size to obtain gauge*

ADDITIONAL MATERIALS
Stitch markers
Scrap yarn or stitch holder

---

circular needle. **Rnd 1 (dec)** [K6, ssk, p1, k3, p1, k2tog, k6] 4 times—76 sts. **Rnd 2 (dec)** [K7, p1, S2KP, p1, k7] 4 times—68 sts. **Rnd 3 (dec)** [K6, ssk, k1, k2tog, k6] 4 times—60 sts. **Rnd 4** Knit. **Rnd 5 (dec)** [K6, S2KP, k6] 4 times—52 sts. **Rnd 6** Knit.
Rnd 7 (dec) [K5, S2KP, k5] 4 times—44 sts. **Rnd 8** Knit. **Rnd 9 (dec)** [K4, S2KP, k4] 4 times—36 sts. **Rnd 10** Knit.
Rnd 11 (dec) [K3, S2KP, k3] 4 times—28 sts.
Rnd 12 Knit.
Rnd 13 (dec) [K2, S2KP, k2] 4 times—20 sts.
Rnd 14 Knit.

Rnd 15 (dec) [K2tog] to end—10 sts.
Cut yarn and draw through rem sts.

Mittens (make 2)

Cuff

With smaller dpn, cast on 26 sts. Join, taking care not to twist sts. Place marker (pm) for beg of rnd and slip marker every rnd.

Next (rib) rnd *[K1, p2] 4 times, k1; rep from * once more. Rep rib rnd until cuff measures 3"/7.5cm from beg. Change to larger needles.

Begin Chart

Note stitch count changes in chart rnds.

Next (set-up) rnd [K4, pm, p2, k1, p2, pm, k4] twice.

Next rnd [K to marker, sl marker, work chart rnd 1, sl marker] twice, k to end of rnd. Cont to work chart in this manner through rnd 8.

Thumb Gusset

Next (inc) rnd Work in pat as established over 13 sts, pm for gusset, M1, pm for gusset, work to end of rnd.

Work 1 rnd even, slipping markers.

Next (inc) rnd Work to first gusset marker, sl marker, M1, k to next gusset marker M1, sl marker, work to end of round. Work 1 rnd even, slipping markers.

Next (inc) rnd Work to first gusset marker, sl marker, M1, k to next gusset marker M1, sl marker, work to end of round.

Work 1 rnd even.

Rep last 2 rnds twice more—7 sts between gusset markers.

(continued on page 32)

Flowered Hat and Wristers

◄■■■ ▭

Sizes
Sized for Small, Medium, Large. Shown in size Medium.

Measurements
- **Hat Circumference** 18 (20, 22)"/45.5 (51, 56)cm
- **Wrister Circumference** 6½ (7½, 8)"/16.5 (19, 20.5)cm

Gauges
20 sts and 28 rnds to 4"/10cm over St st using size 8 (5mm) circular needle.
22 sts and 32 rnds to 4"/10cm over St st using size 5 (3.75mm) dpns.
Take time to check your gauges.

Stitch Glossary
M1 (make 1) Insert left needle from front to back into the horizontal strand between the last st worked and the next st on left needle. Knit this strand through the back loop to twist the st.
M1R (make 1 right) Insert left needle from back to front into the horizontal strand between the last st worked and the next st on left needle. Knit this strand through the front loop to twist the st.

Hat
With circular needle and MC, cast on 88 (100, 108) sts. Join, taking care not to twist sts on needle and pm for beg of rnds. Work in k2, p2 rib for 1"/2.5cm, inc 2 (0, 2) sts evenly spaced around last rnd—90 (100, 110) sts. Cont in St st until piece measures 5 (5½, 6)"/12.5 (14, 15)cm from beg.

Shape Crown
Note Change to dpns when sts no longer comfortably fit on circular needle.
Rnd 1 [K7, SK2P] 9 (10, 11) times—72 (80, 88) sts.
Rnds 2–4 Knit.
Rnd 5 [K5, SK2P] 9 (10, 11) times—54 (60, 66) sts.
Rnds 6–8 Knit

Rnd 9 [K3, SK2P] 9 (10, 11) times—36 (40, 44) sts.
Rnd 10 Knit.
Rnd 11 [K1, SK2P] 9 (10, 11) times—18 (20, 22) sts.
Rnd 12 Knit.
Rnd 13 K 0 (1, 0), *k1, k2tog; rep from * around, end k 0 (1, 1)—12 (14, 15) sts.
Cut yarn leaving a 8"/20.5cm tail and thread through rem sts. Pull tog tightly and secure end.

Wristers (make 2)
With size 5 (3.75mm) dpns and MC, cast on 32 (36, 40) sts dividing sts over 3 needles. Join, taking care not to twist sts on needles and pm for beg of rnds. Work in k2, p2 rib for 10 (12, 14) rnds.
Next (inc) rnd Knit, inc 4 (6, 6) sts evenly spaced—36 (42, 46) sts.
Cont in St st and work even for 7 (8, 9) rnds.

Thumb Gusset
Rnd 1 K17 (20, 22), pm, k2, pm, k17 (20, 22).
Rnd 2 K to first marker, sl marker, M1, k to next marker, M1R, sl marker, k to end—38 (44, 48) sts.
Rnd 3 Knit. Rep last 2 rnds 4 (5, 5) times more—46 (54, 58) sts. Knit next 5 rnds.

Hand
Next (joining) rnd K17 (20, 22), place 12 (14, 14) thumb sts on scrap yarn, cast on 2 sts, k17 (20, 22) sts—36 (42, 46) sts. Knit next 5 rnds. Cont in k1, p1 rib for 4 rnds. Bind off in rib.

Thumb Opening
Place 12 (14, 14) thumb gusset sts over 2 needles.
Next rnd Join yarn and knit across sts, then with 3rd needle pick up and k 1 st in first cast-on st of hand, pm, pick up and k 1 st in last cast-on st of hand—14 (16, 16) sts. Divide sts evenly over 3 dpns. Join and pm for beg of rnds. Knit next 2 rnds.
Next (dec) rnd K to 2 sts before first marker, ssk, sl marker, k2tog, k to end—12 (14, 14) sts. Knit next rnd. Cont in k1, p1 rib for 4 rnds. Bind off in rib.

Flowers (make 3)
With CC, ch 5. Join ch with a sl st forming a ring.
Rnd 1 (RS) *Ch 6, sc in ring; rep from * around 4 times more—5 ch-6 lps.
Rnd 2 *Work (sc, 5 dc, sc) in next ch-6 lp; rep from * around 4 times more, join rnd with a sl st in first sc—5 petals.
Rnd 3 *Ch 6, sc in ring between next 2 sc of rnd 1; rep from * around 4 times more, join rnd with a sl st in first sc—5 ch-6 lps.
Rnd 4 Rep rnd 2.
Rnd 5 Skip first sc of rnd 1, *ch 6, sc in ring between next 2 sc of rnd 1, skip next 2 sc of rnd 1; rep from * around 4 times more, join rnd with a sl st in first sc—5 ch-6 lps. Fasten off.

Finishing
Sew one flower each to hat and wristers. Tack down each petal of rnds 2 and 4.

The Midas Touch Capelet and Hat

■■□□

Sizes
Hat One Size
Cowl Small, Medium, Large, X-Large. Shown in size small.

Measurements
Hat
- Head circumference 20½"/52cm
- Length 7"/18cm

Cowl
- Width at lower edge 38 (43, 48, 53)"/96.5 (109, 122, 134.5)cm
- Length (without neck edge rolled) 16 (16½, 17, 17½)"/40.5 (41.5, 43, 44.5)cm

Gauge
16 sts and 18 rows to 4"/10cm over double seed st using size 10 (6mm) and one strand each of A and B held tog.
Take time to check your gauge.

Stitch Glossary
Double Seed Stitch
(over an even number of sts)
Row 1 (RS) *K1, p1; rep from * to end.
Row 2 K the knit sts and p the purl sts.
Row 3 *P1, k1; rep from * to end.
Row 4 K the knit sts and p the purl sts.
Rep rows 1–4 for double seed st.

Hat
Brim
With straight needles and one strand each of A and B held tog, cast on 16 sts. Work in double seed st until piece measures 20½"/52cm from beg. Bind off. Sew cast-on edge to bound-off edge.

Crown
With RS facing, dpn and one strand each of A and B held tog, pick up and k 80 sts along one long edge of brim. Divide sts evenly over 4 dpn—20 sts on each needle. Place marker for beg of rnd. Knit 1 rnd.
Dec rnd [Ssk, k to last 2 sts on needle, k2tog] 4 times—2 sts dec'd on each dpn, 8 sts dec'd in total.

What you'll need:

Hat
YARN (4)
1¾oz/50g, 120yd/110m of any worsted weight wool tweed in golden green (A)
1¾oz/50g, 225yd/206m of any worsted weight mohair blend in olive (B)
KNITTING NEEDLES
One pair size 10 (6mm) needles *or size to obtain gauge*
One set (5) size 10 (6mm) double-pointed needles (dpn)

Cowl
YARN (4)
5¼oz/150g, 360yd/330m (7oz/200g, 480yd/440m; 7oz/200g, 480yd/440m; 8¾oz/250g, 600yd/550m) of any worsted weight wool tweed in golden green (A)
3½oz/100g, 450yd/412m (5¼oz/150g, 675yd/618m; 5¼oz/150g, 675yd/618m; 7oz/200g, 900yd/824m) of any worsted weight mohair blend in olive (B)
KNITTING NEEDLES
One pair size 10 (6mm) needles *or size to obtain gauge*
One size 10 (6mm) circular needle, 24"/60cm long
ADDITIONAL MATERIALS
Stitch markers

Rep dec rnd every other rnd 8 times more—2 sts rem on each dpn, 8 sts in rnd.
Cut yarn, leaving long tail. Thread tail through rem sts.

Cowl
Body
With straight needles and one strand each of A and B held tog, cast on 28 (28, 30, 30) sts. Work in double seed st for 38 (43, 48, 53)"/96.5 (109, 122, 134.5)cm. Bind off. Sew cast-on edge to bound-off edge for center back seam.

Yoke
With RS facing, circular needle and one strand each of A and B held tog, beg at center back seam, pick up and k 152 (172, 192, 212) sts evenly along edge of body. Place marker (pm) for beg of rnd.
Next rnd K30 (35, 40, 45), pm, k16, pm, k60 (70, 80, 90), pm, k16, pm, k 30 (35, 40, 45).
Next (dec) rnd [K to 2 sts before next marker, k2tog, sl marker, ssk] 4 times, k to end of rnd—144 (164, 184, 204) sts. Cont in St st (k every rnd), rep dec rnd every other rnd 4 (6, 8, 10) times more—112 (116, 120, 124) sts. Work even until yoke measures 9 (9½, 9½, 10)"/23 (24, 24, 25.5)cm from picked-up rnd. Bind off loosely.

Embellished Elf Hat & Wristers

Sizes
Sized for Small, Medium, Large. Shown in size Medium.

Measurements
Hat
- Circumference 18 (20, 22)"/45.5 (51, 56)cm

Wrister
- Circumference 6½ (7½, 8)"/16.5 (19, 20.5)cm

Gauge
14 sts and 22 rnds to 4"/10cm over St st using size 9 (5.5mm) dpns.
Take time to check your gauge.

Stitch Glossary
M1 (make 1) Insert left needle from front to back into the horizontal strand between the last st worked and the next st on left needle. Knit this strand through the back loop to twist the st.

M1R (make 1 right) Insert left needle from back to front into the horizontal strand between the last st worked and the next st on left needle. Knit this strand through the front loop to twist the st.

Hat
Crown
With dpn and MC, cast on 9 sts, leaving a long tail for sewing. Divide sts over 3 needles. Join, taking care not to twist sts on needles and pm for beg of rnds.
Rnd 1 Knit. **Rnd 2** [K1, M1, k2] 3 times—12 sts. **Rnd 3** [Sl 1, k3] 3 times.
Rnd 4 [K1, M1, k3] 3 times—15 sts.
Rnd 5 [Sl 1, k4] 3 times. **Rnd 6** [K1, M1, k4] 3 times—18 sts. **Rnd 7** [Sl 1, k5] 3 times. **Rnd 8** [K1, M1, k5] 3 times—21 sts. **Rnd 9** [Sl 1, k6] 3 times. **Rnd 10** [K1, M1, k6] 3 times—24 sts. **Rnd 11** [Sl 1, k7] 3 times. **Rnd 12** [K1, M1, k7] 3 times—27 sts. **Rnd 13** [Sl 1, k8] 3 times. **Rnd 14** [K1, M1, k8] 3 times—30 sts. **Rnd 15** [Sl 1, k9] 3 times. Cont to work in this manner, inc 3 sts every other rnd and working 1 more st

between sl sts every other rnd until there are 63 (72, 78) sts on dpns. Cont to work as foll:
Next rnd *Sl 1, k20 (23, 25); rep from * around.
Next rnd Knit. Rep last 2 rnds until piece measures 10 (10½, 11)"/25.5 (26.5, 28)cm from beg.

I-Cord Edging
With RS facing and A, cast 3 sts onto LH needle. Work I-cord edging as foll: *with A, k2, then k2tog tbl (last A st and first MC st on LH needle); place the 3 sts on RH needle just knitted onto LH needle; rep from * until 3 sts rem. Bind off rem 3 sts.

Finishing
Thread beg tail in tapestry needle. Weave tail around opening at top of crown. Pull tog tightly and secure end. Sew ends of I-cord edging tog.

Embroidery
Referring to diagram, use B to embroider three 6-petal lazy daisy stitch flowers on front of hat. Using C, embroider two lazy daisy stitch leaves for each flower. Using D,

embroider a 5-wrap bullion knot in center of each flower.

Tassel
Cut four 9"/23cm strands each of MC, A and B. Use yarn needle to thread strands through top of hat. Tie strands in a square knot.

Wristers (make 2)
With dpns and A, cast on 24 (28, 28) sts, dividing sts over 3 needles. Join, taking care not to twist sts on needles and pm for beg of rnds. Work in k2, p2 rib for 3 (3½, 3½)"/7.5 (9, 9)cm, dec 2 (2, 0) sts evenly spaced—22 (26, 28) sts. Change to MC. Cont in St st and work even for 4 (5, 5) rnds.

Thumb Gusset
Rnd 1 K11 (13, 14), pm, M1, M1R, pm, k11 (13, 14)—24 (28, 30) sts. **Rnd 2** Knit. **Rnd 3** K to first marker, sl marker, M1R, k to next marker, M1, sl marker, k to end—26 (30, 32) sts. **Rnd 4** Knit. Rep last two rnds, 3 (3, 4) times more—32 (36, 40) sts. **Next rnd** K11 (13, 14), bind off next 10 (10, 12) sts, k to end.

Hand
Knit 4 rnds over 22 (26, 28) sts. Cont in k1, p1 rib for 4 (6, 6) rnds. Bind off losely in rib.

Finishing
Embroidery
Referring to diagram, use B to embroider one 5-petal lazy daisy stitch flower to front of each wrister. Using C, embroider two or three lazy daisy stitch leaves for each flower. Using D, embroider a 5-wrap bullion knot in center of each flower.

5-Petal flower

6-Petal flower

Stitch key
- Lazy daisy st
- 5-Wrap bullion knot

Color key
- ☐ Light olive (B)
- ◻ Teal green (C)
- ■ Dark pink (D)

Good as Gold Ribbed Cowl and Hat

⬛◼️▢▢

Measurements
Hat
- **Head circumference** 21½"/54.5cm
- **Length (with folded brim)** 8½"/21.5cm

Cowl
- **Circumference** 31"/78.5cm
- **Length** 12"/30.5cm

Gauges
Hat
18 sts and 27 rnds to 4"/10cm over St st using larger needles.

Cowl
17 sts and 24 rnds to 4"/10cm over rib pat using size 7 (4.5mm) needle.
Take time to check your gauges.

Stitch Glossary
Rib Pattern (over a multiple of 11 sts)
Rnd 1 *K5, p1, k5; rep from * around.
Rep rnd 1 for rib pat.

Hat
Brim
With smaller dpn, cast on 96 sts. Divide sts evenly over 4 needles (24 sts on each needle). Join, taking care not to twist sts. Place marker for beg of rnd and slip marker every rnd. Work in k2, p2 rib for 7"/18cm. Change to

larger dpns and work in St st (**Note** This is the wrong side of hat) for 3"/7.5cm.

Shape Crown
Dec rnd 1 [K14, k2tog] 6 times—90 sts. K 1 rnd.
Dec rnd 2 [K13, k2tog] 6 times—84 sts. K 1 rnd. Rep last 2 rnds, working 1 less st

between decs every dec rnd, 3 times more—66 sts.
Cont to dec 6 sts as before *every* rnd 10 times—6 sts. K 1 rnd. Cut yarn, draw through rem sts and secure.

Finishing
Turn hat inside out so that purl side of crown shows. Fold ribbed brim twice to right side (see photo).

Cowl
Note
Cowl is knit in the round on the wrong side, then folded in half on the right side.

Cast on 132 sts. Join, taking care not to twist sts.
Place marker for beg of rnd and slip marker every rnd.
Work in rib pat for 24"/61cm. Bind off.

Finishing
Fold cowl in half so that the purl side shows.

Lacy Eyelet Hat and Scarf

Sizes

Hat is sized for Child's, Women's,
X-small/Small, Women's Medium/Large.
Shown in Women's X-small/Small.

Measurements

- **Head circumference** 16 (17½, 19¼)"/40.5
(44.5, 48.5)cm (unstretched)
- **Scarf** 8" x 58½"/20.5cm x 147cm

Gauge

20 sts and 24 rows to 4"/10cm over eyelet pat
foll chart using size 8 (5mm) needles.
Take time to check your gauge.

Hat

With circular needle, cast on 80 (88, 96)
stitches. Join, taking care not to twist sts on
needle. Place marker for end of rnd and sl
marker every rnd.
Work in k1, p1 rib for 1¾"/4.5cm. Work in St st
for 3 rnds.
Work eyelet pat chart until piece measures 5
(5½, 6)"/12.5 (14, 15)cm from beg.
Note Transfer sts to dpn when there are not
enough to fit on circular needle.

Shape Top

Rnd 1 K6, k2tog; rep from * around—70
(77,84) sts.
Rnd 2 Knit.
Rnd 3 *K5, k2tog; rep from * around—60
(66,72) sts.
Rnd 4 Knit.

Rnd 5 *K4, k2tog; rep from * around—50
(55,60) sts.
Rnd 6 *K3, k2tog; rep from * around—40 (44,
48) sts.
Rnd 7 Knit.
Rnd 8 *K2, k2tog; rep from * around—30 (33,
36) sts.
Rnd 9 Knit.
Rnd 10 *K1, k2tog; rep from * around—20 (22,
24) sts.
Rnd 11 Knit.
Rnd 12 *K2tog; rep from * around—10 (11,12)
sts.
Cut yarn leaving a 12"/30cm tail, thread
through remaining sts, cinch tightly to close.

Scarf

Cast on 45 sts. Work in k1, p1 rib for
2½"/6.5cm ending with a RS row.

Next row (WS) Cont rib over first 9 sts, p into
front and back of next st, p26, cont rib over
last 9 sts—46 sts.
Next row (RS) Cont rib over 9 sts, k28, cont
rib to end.
Next row Cont rib over 9 sts, p28, cont rib to
end. Keeping first and last 9 sts in rib, work
center 28 sts in eyelet pat chart until piece
measures 56"/143.5cm from beg, end with a
chart row 8.
Work k1, p1 rib over all sts for 2½"/6.5cm.
Bind off in rib.

EYELET PATTERN

4-st repeat

STITCH KEY

☐ K on RS, p on WS

☒ K2tog

⊙ Yo

Buttoned Capelet and Beret

Measurements

Beret
- **Diameter** approx 10"/25.5cm

Capelet
- **Width at lower edge (buttoned)** approx 60"/152cm
- **Length from center back neck (without collar)** 11¼"/28.5cm

Gauges

Beret

12 sts and 20 rnds to 4"/10cm over k3, p3 rib using size 10 (6mm) needles.

Capelet

16 sts and 20 rows to 4"/10cm over k3, p2 rib using size 10 (6mm) needles.
Take time to check your gauges.

Stitch Glossary

K3, P2 Rib (over a multiple of 5 sts plus 2)
Row 1 (RS) P2, *k3, p2; rep from * to end.
Row 2 K2, *p3, k2; rep from * to end. Rep rows 1 and 2 for k3, p2 rib.

Decrease Wedge (over 7 sts)
Row 1 (RS) P2, k3, p2.
Row 2 K2, p3, k2.
Dec row 3 P2, SK2P, p2—5 sts.
Row 4 K2, p1, k2.
Dec row 5 P1, p2tog, p2—4 sts.
Row 6 K4.
Dec row 7 P1, p3tog—2 sts.
Row 8 P2.
Note The decrease wedge rows 3-7 are worked over the designated ribs at intervals for wedge shape decreasing. The other rows are given for clarity.

What you'll need:

Beret
YARN (5)
3½oz/100g, 120yd/110m of any bulky weight wool tweed yarn in fuchsia

KNITTING NEEDLES
One set (5) size 10 (6mm) dpn *or size to obtain gauge*

ADDITIONAL MATERIALS
Size I/9 (5.5mm) crochet hook

Capelet
YARN
12¼oz/350g, 420yd/385m of any bulky weight wool tweed yarn in fuchsia

KNITTING NEEDLES
Size 10 (6mm) circular needle, 36"/90cm long *or size to obtain gauge*
One pair size 10 (6mm) needles

ADDITIONAL MATERIALS
Five 1⅛-inch/27mm buttons
Stitch markers
Stitch holders

Sloped Cast On
On the row previous to the cast-on, sl the last st wyib on RS, wyif on WS; then at beg of next cast-on row, use cable cast-on method with two needles.

Beret

Beg at center, with crochet hook, ch 4, join with sl st to first ch to form ring. Ch 1, work 11 sc in ring.

Rnd 1 With loop on hook, pick up 3 more loops in the next 3 sc and sl from end of hook to first dpn; then pick up 4 loops and sl to 2nd dpn; pick up 4 more loops and sl to 3rd dpn—12 sts with 4 sts on each dpn. Weave in a contrast yarn to carry along and mark the beg of rnds.

Rnd 2 Needle 1: [Kfb, pfb] twice; **Needle 2:** [kfb, pfb] twice; **Needle 3:** [kfb, pfb] twice—24 sts.

Rnds 3 and 4 [K2, p2] 6 times.

Rnd 5 Needle 1: [K2, pfb, p1] twice; **Needle 2:** [k2, pfb, p1] twice; **Needle 3:** [k2, pfb, p1] twice—30 sts.

Rnd 6 [K2, p3] 6 times.

Rnd 7 Needle 1: [K2, p1, pfb, p1] twice; **Needles 2 and 3:** work same as Needle 1—36 sts.

Rnd 8 [K2, p4] 6 times.

Rnd 9 Needle 1: *K2, p1, (p1, k1) into next st, p2*; rep between *'s once more; **Needles 2 and 3:** work same as Needle 1—42 sts.

Rnd 10 [K2, p2, k1, p2] 6 times.

Rnd 11 Needle 1: *K2, p2, M1, k1, M1, p2*; rep between *'s once more; **Needles 2 and 3:** work same as Needle 2—54 sts.

Rnd 12 [K2, p2, k3, p2] 6 times.

Rnd 13 Needle 1: *Kfb, k1, p2, k3, p2*; rep between *'s once more; **Needles 2 and 3:** work same as Needle 1—60 sts.

Rnd 14 [K3, p2] 12 times.

Rnd 15 Needle 1: *K3, pfb, p1, k3, p2*; rep

between *'s once more; **Needles 2 and 3:** work same as Needle 1—66 sts.

Rnd 16 [K3, p3, k3, p2] 6 times.

Rnd 17 Needle 1: *K3, p3, k3, pfb, p1*; rep between *'s once more; **Needles 2 and 3:** work same as Needle 1—72 sts.

Rnd 18 *K3, p3; rep from * around. At this point, divide sts onto 4 needles with 18 sts on each needle and cont to work in rnds of k3, p3 rib for 18 rnds more. Bind off knitwise. Do not fasten off. Turn hat to the WS and with loop on hook, ch 1, and working into front loops of the bound-off edge only, *work 2 hdc, skip 1 st; rep from * around, join and fasten off.

Note Adjust the number of hdc for the desired head circumference.

Finishing

Immerse hat in cold water and roll in a towel to squeeze out excess moisture. Then insert a 10"/25.5cm dinner plate into hat and leave to dry to form the beret shape.

Capelet

Back Segment

With size 10 (6mm) straight needles, cast on 47 sts.

Row 1 (RS) P2, [k3, p2] 9 times.

Row 2 (WS) Cast on 5 sts, k2, *p3, k2; rep from * to end—52 sts.

Row 3 (RS) Cast on 5 sts, p2, *k3, p2; rep from * to end—57 sts.

Rows 4, 6 and 8 Rep row 2.

Rows 5, 7 and 9 Rep row 3—87 sts.

Turn to WS, cast on 15 sts and leave 102 sts on hold on the circular needle.

Left Front Segment

With size 10 (6mm) straight needles, cast on 32 sts.

Row 1 (WS) P3, [k1, p1] twice, k1, p2, [k2, p3] 4 times, k2.

Row 2 (RS) Cast on 5 sts, p2, [k3, p2] 5 times, sl 2 wyib, [p1, k1] twice, p1, sl 3 wyib—37 sts.

Row 3 (WS) P3, [k1, p1] twice, k1, p2 (10-st band); k2, *p3, k2; rep from * to end.

Row 4 (RS) Cast on 5 sts, *p2, k3; rep from * to 2 sts before band, p2, work sl 2 wyib, [p1, k1] twice, p1, sl 3 wyib—42 sts.

Rows 5 and 7 Rep row 3.

Row 6 Rep row 4—47 sts.

Row 8 Rep row 4—52 sts.

Row 9 Rep row 3.

Turn to the RS and cast on 13 sts, cut yarn and pm, then sl these 65 sts to left end of the circular needle with the marker between front and back sts.

Right Front

With size 10 (6mm) straight needles, cast on 32 sts.

Row 1 (RS) Sl 3 wyib, p1, [k1, p1] twice, sl 2 wyib; p2, [k3, p2] 5 times.

Row 2 (WS) Cast on 5 sts, *k2, p3; rep from * to last 2 sts before band, k2, p2, k1, [p1, k1] twice, p3—37 sts.

Row 3 Sl 3 wyib, p1, [k1, p1] twice, sl 2 wyib; work in rib to end.

Row 4 Rep row 2—42 sts.

Row 5 Rep row 3.

Row 6 Rep row 2—47 sts.

Buttonhole row 7 (RS) Sl 3 wyib, p1, k1, (yo) twice, k2tog (for vertical buttonhole row 1), work even to end.

Buttonhole row 8 Cast on 5 sts, *k2, p3; rep from * to 2 sts before band, k2, p2, k1, p1, sl the double yo and yo twice again (for buttonhole row 2), work to end.

Buttonhole row 9 Sl 3, p1, k1, k1 through the yo's (buttonhole row 3), work to end—52 sts. Turn and cast on 13 sts at beg of next row, then place marker. Cast on 15 more sts (for back). Sl these 80 sts to circular needle in position for right front.

Cut yarn.

Capelet

Rejoin yarn from the RS and work as foll:

Row 1 (RS) Work 65 sts of right front, sl marker, work 117 sts of back, sl marker, work 65 sts of left front—247 sts. **Row 2** Work even.

Row 3 Work 20 sts, work dec wedge row 3 over next 7 sts, work to 4 sts before marker, *k2tog, place new marker, k1, SKP removing previous marker*; work 34 sts, work dec wedge row 3 over 7 sts, work 33 sts, work dec wedge row 3 over next 7 sts, work to 1 st before marker; rep between *'s once, work 34 sts, work dec wedge row 3 over 7 sts, work 20 sts—235 sts.

Row 4 Work even, working wedge row 4 over the 4 dec'd segments.

Row 5 Work even, working wedge row 5 over the 4 dec'd segments—231 sts.

Row 6 Work even, working wedge row 6 over the 4 dec'd segments.

Row 7 Working row 7 of the dec wedge over the 4 dec'd segments, AND, work the side dec's as foll: *work to 2 sts before marker, k2tog, sl marker, k1, SKP; rep from * once more, work to end—219 sts.

Row 8 Work even.

Row 9 Work 25 sts, *work dec wedge row 3 over next 7 sts*, work to first marker, sl marker, work 25 sts; rep between *'s once, work 43 sts; rep between *'s once, work to 2nd marker, sl marker, work 25 sts; rep between *'s once, work 25 sts—211 sts.

Row 10 Work even, working wedge row 4 over the 4 dec'd segments.

Row 11 Working row 5 of the dec wedge over the 4 dec'd segments, work the side dec's as foll: *work to 2 sts before marker, k2tog, sl marker, k1, SKP; rep from * once more, work to end—203 sts.

Row 12 Work even, working wedge row 6 over the 4 dec'd segments.

Row 13 Work in pat, working wedge row 7 over the 4 dec'd segments—195 sts.

Row 14 Work even.

Buttonhole row 15 Sl 3, p1, k1, (yo) twice, k2tog, work 23 sts, *work dec wedge row 3 over the next 7 sts*; work to 2 sts before marker, k2tog, sl marker, k1, SKP, work 11 sts; rep between *'s, work 53 sts; rep between *'s, work 11 sts, k2tog, sl marker, k1, SKP, work 11 sts; rep between *'s, work to end—183 sts.

Row 16 Work in pat, working wedge row 4 over the 4 dec'd segments AND work buttonhole row 2 at end of row.

Row 17 Work in pat working wedge row 5 over the 4 dec'd segments AND work buttonhole row 3 at beg of row—179 sts.

Row 18 Rep row 12.

Row 19 Work in pat working wedge row 7 over the 4 dec'd segments and dec 2 sts at markers as before—167 sts.

Row 20 Work even.

Row 21 Work 20 sts, *work dec wedge row 3 over next 7 sts*, work 33 sts; rep between *'s once, work 33 sts; rep between *'s once, work 33 sts; rep between *'s once, work 20 sts—159 sts.

Row 22 Rep row 10.

Row 23 Rep row 11—151 sts.

Row 24 Rep row 12.

Row 25 Rep row 13—143 sts.

Row 26 Work even.

Row 27 Work to 2 sts before marker, k2tog, sl marker, k1, SKP, work 3 sts, *work dec wedge row 3 over next 7 sts*, work 43 sts; rep between *'s once, work 3 sts, k2tog, sl marker, k1, SKP, work to end—135 sts.

Row 28 Work even, working wedge row 4 over the 2 dec'd wedges.

Row 29 Work even, working wedge row 5 over the 2 dec'd segments—133 sts.

Row 30 Work even, working wedge row 6 over the 2 dec'd segments.

Buttonhole row 31 Sl 3, p1, k1, (yo) twice, k2tog, *work to 2 sts before marker, k2tog, sl marker, k1, SKP*, work wedge row 7 over the 2 dec'd segments; rep between *'s once, work to end—125 sts.

Row 32 Work even, working buttonhole row 2 at end of the row. There are 35 sts in right front, 54 sts between markers for back and 36 sts in left front.

Row 33 Work buttonhole row 3 at beg of row, rib to marker, sl marker, rib 9 sts, *work wedge dec row 3 over next 7 sts*, work 23 sts; rep between *'s once, work to end—121 sts.

Row 34 Work even, working wedge row 4 over the 2 dec'd segments.

Shape Neck

Row 35 (RS) Work 10 sts and sl to a st holder, *work to 2 sts before marker, k2tog, sl marker, k1, SKP*, work wedge row 5 over the 2 dec'd segments; rep between *'s once, work to the last 10 sts, sl these sts to holder—95 sts.

Row 36 (WS) Bind off 3 sts, work even to end, working wedge row 6 over the 2 dec'd segments.

Row 37 (RS) Bind off 3 sts, *work to 2 sts before marker, k2tog, sl marker, k1, SKP*; work wedge row 7 over the 2 dec'd segments; rep between *'s once more, work to end—81 sts.

Row 38 Bind off 3 sts, work even to end.

Row 39 Bind off 3 sts, *work to 2 sts before marker, k2tog, sl marker, k1, SKP*; rep between *'s once, work even to end—71 sts.

Rows 40-45 Rep (rows 38 and 39) 3 times—41 sts.

Row 46 Work even.

Row 47 Dec 2 sts at each marker—37 sts. Cut yarn.

Collar

Row 1 (RS) From the RS, sl the first 10 sts to needle, rejoin yarn and pick up and k 15 sts along the shaped collar edge, rib 37 sts from needle, pick up and k 15 sts along the shaped collar, work the 10 sts from holder—87 sts. Cont with established 10 sts for front bands, work 11 rows more in rib.

Next 3 rows Work buttonhole rows 1-3 over the first 10-st band. Work 13 rows even. **Next 3 rows** Work buttonhole rows 1-3 over the first 10-st band. Work 3 rows even. Bind off.

Lower Edge

From RS, pick up and k 1 st in each st along lower edge.
Bind off knitwise.

Finishing

Block to measurements. Sew on buttons.

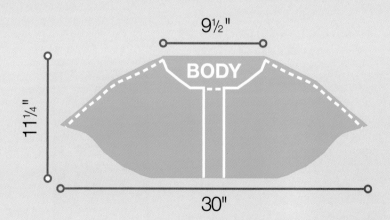

Man's Hat and Striped Scarf

Measurements

Hat
- **Circumference** 21"/53.5cm
- **Length** 8"/20.5cm

Scarf
- **Approximately** 5½ x 65"/14 x 165cm

Gauges

Hat
20 sts and 26 rnds to 4"/10cm over St st using larger needles.

Scarf
30 sts and 26 rows to 4"/10cm over k1, p1 rib using size 7 (4.5mm) needles.
Take time to check your gauges.

Stitch Glossary

K1, P1 Rib
(over an even number of sts)
Row 1 (RS) Sl 1 purlwise, *k1, p1; rep from *, end k1.
Row 2 Sl 1 purlwise, k the knit sts and p the purl sts.
Rep row 2 for k1, p1 rib.

Hat

Notes
1 When working chart pat, carry color not in use loosely on WS of work.
2 When working chart pat, pick up B strand under A strand.

With smaller circular needle and A, cast on 96 sts. Join, being careful not to twist sts and place marker for beg of rnd. *K1, p1; rep from * around for k1, p1 rib until piece measures 1"/2.5cm from beg.
Next rnd *K11, kfb; rep from * around—104 sts. Change to larger needle and B. Knit 2 rounds.

What you'll need:

Hat
YARN (4)
1¾oz/50g, 91yd/87m of any worsted weight wool blend in cadet blue (A) and shadow gray (B)

KNITTING NEEDLES
One each sizes 5 and 7 (3.75 and 4.5mm) circular needles, 16"/40cm long *or size to obtain gauge*
One set (5) size 5 (3.75mm) double-pointed needles (dpns)

ADDITIONAL MATERIALS
4 stitch markers

Striped Scarf
YARN
7oz/200g, 364yd/348m of any worsted weight wool blend in shadow gray (A)
1¾oz/50g, 91yd/87m in cadet blue (B)

KNITTING NEEDLES
One pair size 7 (4.5mm) needles *or size to obtain gauge*

Begin Chart
Work in St st (knit every rnd) foll chart, working 8-st rep 13 times around until rnd 12 of chart is complete. K 2 rnds B. Cut B. Change to A. Cont in St st until cap measures 5"/12.5cm from beg.

Shape Crown
Note Change to dpns when sts no longer fit comfortably on circular needle.
Next rnd *K26, pm, rep from * twice more, k to end of rnd.
Next (dec) rnd *K2tog, k to 2 sts before next marker, ssk, sl marker, rep from * 3 times more—96 sts.

Next rnd Knit.
Rep dec rnd every other rnd 8 times more—32 sts. Then, rep dec rnd *every* rnd 3 times more—8 sts. Cut yarn, leaving a long tail. Thread tail through rem sts twice and pull tight.

Finishing
Block fair isle band gently if necessary.

Scarf

Notes
1 Slip the first st of each row purlwise for an even edge.
2 Carry colors up the side when working stripe sections.

With A, cast on 42 sts. Work in k1, p1 rib for 14 rows, taking care to slip first st each row. Join B. Cont in rib as established, work [2 rows B, 2 rows A] 6 times. Cut B. Cont in pat with A only until piece measures 59½"/151cm from beg. Join B. Work [2 rows B, 2 rows A] 6 times. Cut B. With A, work 12 rows more. Bind off in rib.

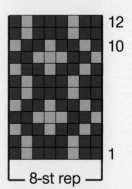

12
10

1

└ 8-st rep ┘

COLOR KEY
■ Cadet blue (A)
■ Shadow (B)

Do the Twist
Cabled Cape and Hat

Sizes
Hat Sized for Adult Woman.
Capelet Sized for Small/Medium, Large/X-Large, XX-Large. Shown in size Small/Medium.

Measurements
Hat
- **Circumference** 21"/53cm

Capelet
- **Width at lower edge** 59 (62¾, 66½)"/150 (159, 169)cm
- **Length** 16 (16, 17½)"/40.5 (40.5, 44.5)cm

Gauges
Hat
16 sts and 26 rnds to 4"/10cm over cable pat in section 1 using larger dpn.
Capelet
17 sts and 26 rnds to 4"/10cm over St st using size 9 (5.5mm) needles.
Take time to check your gauges.

Stitch Glossary
K2, P2 Rib (multiple of 4 sts)
Rnd 1 *K2, p2; rep from * around.
Rnd 2 K the knit sts and p the purl sts.
Rep rnd 2 for k2, p2 rib.

10-st LC Sl 5 sts to cn and hold to *front*, k5, k5 from cn.
8-st LC Sl 4 sts to cn and hold to *front*, k4, k4 from cn.
6-st LC Sl 3 sts to cn and hold to *front*, k3, k3 from cn.

4-st LC Sl 2 sts to cn and hold to *front*, k2, k2 from cn.

What you'll need:

Hat
YARN (4)
1¾oz/50g, 109yd/98m of any worsted weight wool tweed
KNITTING NEEDLES
One set (5) each sizes 7 and 9 (4.5 and 5.5mm) double-pointed needles (dpn) *or size to obtain gauge*
ADDITIONAL MATERIALS
Cable needle (cn)
Stitch marker

Capelet
YARN (4)
10½ oz/300g, 654yd/588m (12¼oz/350g, 763yd/686m; 14oz/400g, 872yd/784m) of any worsted weight wool tweed
KNITTING NEEDLES
Two size 9 (5.5mm) circular needles, one each 16"/40cm and 32"/80cm long *or size to obtain gauge*
ADDITIONAL MATERIALS
Cable needle (cn)
Stitch marker

Hat
With smaller dpn, cast on 84 sts. Divide sts evenly over 4 needles (21 sts on each needle). Join, taking care not to twist sts, and place marker for beg of rnd.
Work in k2, p2 rib for 3"/7.5cm.
Change to larger dpn.

Section 1
Rnds 1 and 3 Knit. **Rnds 2 and 4** [K2, p2, k6, p2] 7 times around. **Rnd 5** [K4, 6-st LC, k2] 7 times around. **Rnd 6** Rep rnd 2.
Rep rnds 1–6 twice more. Work rnds 1–5 once more.
Next (dec) rnd [K2, p2, ssk, k2, k2tog, p2] 7 times around—70 sts.

Section 2
Rnd 1 Knit. **Rnds 2 and 4** [K2, p2, k4, p2] 7 times around. **Rnd 3** [K4, 4-st LC, k2] 7 times around. Rep rnds 1–4 once more.
Next (dec) rnd [K4, ssk, k2tog, k2] 7 times around—56 sts.

Section 3
Rnd 1 *K2, p2; rep from * around. **Rnd 2** Knit. Rep rnds 1 and 2 until piece measures 7¾"/19.5cm from beg, end with a rnd 2.
Next (dec) rnd *K2, p2tog; rep from * around—42 sts. Knit 1 rnd.
Next (dec) rnd *K1, ssk; rep from * around—28 sts. Knit 1 rnd.
Next (dec) rnd K2tog around—14 sts.
Cut yarn and thread through rem sts. Pull to close top and secure.

(continued on page 32)

Simple Red Sets

Measurements

Scarf
- Approximately 9 x 66"/23 x 167.5cm

Hat
- Head circumference (at ribbed brim) 17"/43cm
- **Length** 10"/25.5cm

Gauges

- 18 sts and 24 rows to 4"/10cm over St st using larger needles.
- 20 sts and 26 rows to 4"/10cm over St st using smaller needles.

Take time to check your gauges.

Stitch Glossary

K2, P2 Rib
(over a multiple of 4 sts)
Row 1 *K2, p2; rep from * to end.
Row 2 K the knit sts and p the purl sts.
Rep row 2 for k2, p2 rib.

Note

Cut colors not in use for more than 4 rows.

Scarf

With larger needles and A, cast on 40 sts and work 6 rows in k2, p2 rib. Change to St st (k on RS, p on WS) and work 8 rows.

Beg Stripes

Cont in St st as foll:
[2 rows B, 2 rows A] 3 times, 2 rows A, 30 rows B, [2 rows C, 2 rows D] 3 times, 2 rows C, 20 rows A, 2 rows D, 4 rows B, 40 rows C, 4 rows B, [2 rows D, 2 rows A] 3 times, [2 rows C, 2 rows A] 3 times, [2 rows B, 2 rows A] 3 times, 44 rows A, [2 rows A, 2 rows B] 3 times, [2 rows A, 2 rows C] 3 times, [2 rows A, 2 rows D] 3 times, 4 rows B, 40 rows C, 4 rows B, 2 rows D, 20 rows A, [2 rows C, 2 rows D] 3 times, 2 rows C, 30 rows B, 4 rows A, [2 rows B, 2 rows A] 3 times, 6 rows A. Cont with A, work 6 rows in k2, p2 rib. Bind off.

Hat

With smaller needles and A, cast on 90 sts and work 6 rows in k2, p2 rib. Change to St st and work 4 rows.

Beg Stripes

Cont in St st and work in stripes as foll:
[2 rows C, 2 rows A] 3 times, 2 rows A, join B to complete hat, AT THE SAME TIME, when piece measures 7¼"/18.5cm from beg, end with WS row, shape crown.

Shape Crown

Row 1 (RS) *K7, k2tog; rep from* to end—80 sts.
Row 2 (and all WS rows) Purl.
Row 3 *K6, K2tog; rep from * to end—70 sts.
Row 5 *K5, k2tog; rep from * to end—60 sts.
Row 7 *K4, k2tog; rep from * to end—50 sts.
Row 9 *K3, k2tog; rep from * to end—40 sts.
Row 11 *K2, k2tog; rep from * to end—30 sts.
Row 13 *K1, k2tog; rep from * to end—20 sts.
Row 15 *K2tog; rep from * to end—10 sts.
Row 16 P10. Cut yarn, leaving 12"/30.5cm tail. Thread tapestry needle with tail and draw through rem sts. Sew seam.

Berry Stripes

Measurements

Scarf
- Approximately 9 x 66"/23 x 167.5cm

Hat
- Head circumference (at ribbed brim) 17"/43cm
- Length 11½"/29cm

Gauges

- 18 sts and 24 rows to 4"/10cm over St st using larger needles.
- 21 sts and 31 rows to 4"/10cm over Sl st pat using larger needles.

Take time to check your gauges.

Stitch Glossary

K2, P2 Rib (over a multiple of 4 sts)
Row 1 *K2, p2; rep from * to end.
Row 2 K the knit sts and p the purl sts.
Rep row 2 for k2, p2 rib.

Slip Stitch Pattern (over an odd number of sts)
Row 1 (RS) With B, k1, *sl 1 wyif, k1; rep from * to end.
Row 2 With B, purl.
Row 3 With C, k1, *sl 1 wyib, k1; rep from * to end.
Row 4 With C, purl.
Row 5 With D, k1 *sl 1 wyif, k1; rep from * to end.
Row 6 With D, purl.
Rows 7 and 8 With B, rep rows 3 and 4.

What you'll need:

YARN (4)
3½oz/100g, 220yd/201m of any worsted weight wool in rose (A), fuchsia (B), pale pink (C), and brown (D)

KNITTING NEEDLES
One pair each size 7 and 8 (4.5 and 5mm) needles *or size to obtain gauge*

Rows 9 and 10 With C, rep rows 1 and 2.
Rows 11 and 12 With D, rep rows 3 and 4. Rep rows 1-12 for slip st pat.

Note

Cut colors not in use for more than 4 rows.

Scarf

With larger needles and A, cast on 40 sts and work 6 rows in k2, p2 rib.
Next row (RS) Inc 1 st, k39—41 sts. Purl 1 row.

Beg Pat
*Work rows 1-12 of sl st pat 3 times. Change to A and St st and work 12 rows. Rep from * 8 times more. Work rows 1-12 of sl st pat 3 times. K 1 row A.
Next (dec) row (WS) P39, p2tog—40 sts. Cont with A, change to k2, p2 rib and work 6 rows. Bind off.

Cap

With smaller needles and A, cast on 90 sts and work 6 rows in k2, p2 rib. Change to larger needles.
Next row (RS) Inc 1 st, k89—91 sts. Purl 1 row. Cont with St st and A, work 2 rows.

Beg Pat
Work rows 1-12 of sl st pat 6 times.

Shape Crown
With A shape crown as foll:
Row 1 (RS) *K5, k2tog; rep from * to end—78 sts.
Row 2 and all WS rows Purl.
Row 3 *K4, k2tog; rep from * to end—65 sts.
Row 5 *K3, k2tog; rep from * to end—52 sts.
Row 7 *K2, k2tog—39 sts.
Row 9 *K1, k2tog; rep from * to end—26 sts.
Row 11 (K2tog) 13 times—13 sts.
Row 12 P13. Cut yarn, leaving 12"/30.5cm tail. Thread tapestry needle with tail and draw through rem sts. Sew seam.

PHOTOGRAPH BY DAVID LAZURUS

Teal Stripes

What you'll need:

YARN (4)
3½oz/100g, 220yd/201m of any worsted weight wool in dark gray heather (A), blue heather (B), light blue heather (C), aqua (D)

KNITTING NEEDLES
One pair each size 7 and 8 (4.5 and 5mm) needles *or size to obtain gauge*

Measurements

Scarf
- Approximately 9 x 66"/23 x 167.5cm

Hat
- Head circumference (at ribbed brim) 17"/43cm
- **Length** 10"/25.5cm

Gauges
- 18 sts and 24 rows to 4"/10cm over St st using larger needles.
- 20 sts and 26 rows to 4"/10cm over St st using smaller needles.

Take time to check your gauges.

Scarf and Cap
Work same as Red Stripes (see page 24).

Gold Stripes

■■□□

What you'll need:

YARN [4]
3½oz/100g, 220yd/201m of any worsted weight wool in yellow (A), orange (B), pale yellow (C), olive green (D

KNITTING NEEDLE
One pair each size 7 and 8 (4.5 and 5mm) needles *or size to obtain gauge*

PHOTOGRAPH BY DAVID LAZURUS

Measurements
Scarf
- Approximately 9 x 66"/23 x 167.5cm

Hat
- Head circumference (at ribbed brim) 17"/43cm
- **Length** 11½"/29cm

Gauges
- 18 sts and 24 rows to 4"/10cm over St st using larger needles.
- 21 sts and 31 rows to 4"/10cm over Sl st pat using larger needles.

Take time to check your gauges.

Scarf and Cap
Work same as Berry Stripes (see page 26).

Purple Stripes

Measurements

Scarf
- Approximately 9 x 66"/23 x 167.5cm

Cap
- **Head circumference** (at ribbed brim) 17"/43cm
- **Length** 7¼"/18.5cm

Gauge

- 18 sts and 24 rows to 4"/10cm over St st using larger needles.
- 20 sts and 26 rows to 4"/10cm over St st using smaller needles.

Take time to check your gauges.

Stitch Glossary

K2, P2 Rib
(over a multiple of 4 sts)
Row 1 *K2, p2; rep from * to end.
Row 2 K the knit sts and p the purl sts.
Rep row 2 for k2, p2 rib.

Note

Cut colors not in use for more than 4 rows.

Scarf

With larger needles and A, cast on 40 sts and work 6 rows in k2, p2 rib. Change to St st (k on RS, p on WS) and work 8 rows.

Beg Stripes
Cont in St st as foll: [4 rows B, 4 rows A] twice,

What you'll need:

YARN (4)
3½oz/100g, 220yd/201m of any worsted weight wool in purple (A),
gray heather (B) lt purple heather (C),
gray/purple heather (D)

KNITTING NEEDLES
One pair each size 7 and 8 (4.5 and 5mm) needles *or size to obtain gauge*

4 rows B, [2 rows C, 2 rows B] twice, 50 rows C, 12 rows D, 6 rows A, 12 rows D, 2 rows B, [2 rows D, 2 rows B] 3 times, [2 rows C, 2 rows B] 3 times, [2 rows A, 2 rows B] 3 times, 20 rows more with B, 40 rows D, 22 rows B, [2 rows A, 2 rows B] 3 times, [2 rows C, 2 rows B] 3 times, [2 rows D, 2 rows B] 3 times, 12 rows D, 6 rows A, 12 rows D, 50 rows C, [2 rows B, 2 rows C] twice, [4 rows B, 4 rows A] twice, 4 rows B, 8 rows A. Cont with A, change to k2, p2 rib and work 6 rows. Bind off.

Cap

With smaller needles and A, cast on 90 sts and work 6 rows in k2, p2 rib.

Beg Stripes
Change to St st and work stripes as foll:
[2 rows B, 2 rows A] 3 times, [2 rows B, 2 rows D] 3 times, [2 rows B, 2 rows C] 3 times, cont in B until cap is complete, *at the same time*, when cap measures 4½"/11.5cm from beg, shape crown.

Shape Crown
Row 1 (RS) *K7, k2tog; rep from* to end—80 sts.
Row 2 (and all WS rows) Purl.
Row 3 *K6, K2tog; rep from * to end—70 sts.
Row 5 *K5, K2tog; rep from * to end—60 sts.
Row 7 *K4, k2tog; rep from * to end—50 sts.
Row 9 *K3, k2tog; rep from * to end—40 sts.
Row 11 *K2, k2tog; rep from * to end—30 sts.
Row 13 *K1, k2tog; rep from * to end—20 sts.
Row 15 *K2tog; rep from * to end—10 sts.
Row 16 P10. Cut yarn, leaving 12"/30.5cm tail. Thread tapestry needle with tail and draw through rem sts. Sew seam.

PHOTOGRAPH BY DAVID LAZURUS

Hand

Next rnd Cont in pat as established to gusset marker, place next 7 sts on scrap yarn or stitch holder for thumb removing markers, work in pat to end of rnd.
Cont in pat until rnd 8 of chart has been completed 4 times—26 sts in rnd.
Rep rnds 1-5 once more—30 sts.

Shape Mitten Top

Rnd 1 (dec) [K3, ssk, p1, k3, p1, k2tog, k3] twice—26 sts.
Rnd 2 (dec) [K4, p1, S2KP, p1, k4] twice—22 sts.

Rnd 3 (dec) [K3, ssk, k1, k2tog, k3] twice—18 sts.
Rnd 4 Knit.
Rnd 5 (dec) [K3, S2KP, k3] twice—14 sts.
Rnd 6 Knit. **Rnd 7 (dec)** [K2, S2KP, k2] twice—10 sts.
Rnd 8 (dec) [Ssk, k1, k2tog] twice—6 sts.
Cut yarn and thread through rem sts. Fasten off.

Thumb

With larger dpn, pick up and k 5 sts along top of thumb opening, place thumb sts onto larger dpn—12 sts.
Distribute evenly on 3 dpn. Work in St st (k every rnd) until thumb is ½"/1.5cm shorter than desired thumb length.

Next (dec) rnd [K2tog] 6 times—6 sts.
Next rnd Knit.
Next (dec) rnd [K2tog] 3 times—3 sts.
Cut yarn and thread through rem sts. Fasten off.

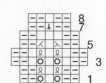

STITCH KEY

□ knit	◎ yo
⊟ purl	⊠ k1 tbl
⊠ k2tog	⊼ S2KP
⊠ ssk	

Cabled Cape and Hat *(continued from page 22)*

Capelet

With longer circular needle, cast on 256 (272, 288) sts. Join rnd taking care not to twist sts. Place marker for beg of rnd and sl marker every rnd.
Work in k2, p2 rib for 3 rnds.
Rnd 1 Knit.
Rnd 2 *K2, p2, k10, p2; rep from * around.
Rep last 2 rnds until piece measures 3"/7.5cm from beg, end with a rnd 2.

Section 1

Rnd 1 *K4, 10-st LC, k2; rep from * around.
Rnds 2, 4, 6, 8 and 10 *K2, p2, k10, p2; rep from * around.
Rnds 3, 5, 7 and 9 Knit.
Rep rnds 1–10 for 2 (2, 3) times more; work rnds 1–6 once more.
Next (dec) rnd *K4, ssk, k6, k2tog, k2; rep from * around—224 (238, 252) sts.
Next rnd *K2, p2, k8, p2; rep from * around.

Section 2

Rnd 1 *K4, 8-st LC, k2; rep from * around.
Rnds 2, 4, 6 and 8 *K2, p2, k8, p2; rep from * around.
Rnds 3, 5 and 7 Knit.
Rnd 9 Rep rnd 1.
Rnd 10 Rep rnd 2.
Next (dec) rnd *K4, ssk, k4, k2tog, k2; rep from * around—192 (204, 216) sts.
Next rnd * K2, p2, k6, p2; rep from * around.

Section 3

Rnd 1 Knit.
Rnds 2, 4 and 6 *K2, p2, k6, p2; rep from * around.
Rnd 3 *K4, 6-st LC, k2; rep from * around.
Rnd 5 Knit.
Rep rnds 1–6 once more.
Next (dec) rnd *K4, ssk, k2, k2tog, k2; rep from * around—160 (170, 180) sts.
Next rnd *K2, p2, k4, p2; rep from * around.

Section 4

Rnd 1 *K4, 4-st LC, k2; rep from * around.
Rnds 2 and 4 *K2, p2, k4, p2; rep from * around.
Rnd 3 Knit.
Rep rnds 1–4 until piece measures approx 13 (13, 14½)"/33 (33, 37)cm from beg, end with a rnd 1.
Next (dec) rnd *K4, ssk, k2tog, k2; rep from * around 128 (136, 144) sts.
Cont in k2, p2 rib for 3"/7.5cm. Bind off all sts purlwise.